For Art's Sake

For Art's Sake

Poems by

Curt G. Curtin

© 2019 Curt G. Curtin. All rights reserved.
This material may not be reproduced in any form, published,
reprinted, recorded, performed, broadcast,
rewritten or redistributed without
the explicit permission of Curt G. Curtin.
All such actions are strictly prohibited by law.

Cover design by Shay Culligan

Cover art "Assumption" by Marjory Lehan

ISBN: 978-1-950462-45-2

Kelsay Books Inc.

kelsaybooks.com

502 S 1040 E, A119
American Fork, Utah 84003

To Dee,

my best friend and the love of my life

Acknowledgments

The following poems in this collection
have been published previously:

"after Auden's *Musée des Beaux Arts*," First Prize, Frank O'Hara Award, Worcester County Poetry Association, 2010; published in *The Worcester Review,* Vol XXXI, 1-2, 2010. Also received the editor's 2010 nomination for a Pushcart Prize.

"Katie and the Poet," *The Worcester Review,* Vol. XXIX, 1-2, 2008. Also received the editor's 2008 nomination for a Pushcart Prize.

"When I Try For Color," *Ballard Street Poetry Journal, 2006.*

"Eldersong," in *Why Education in the Later Years,* Lexington Books, Lowy and O'Connor, *1986.*

All royalties from the sale of this book will be donated to WGBH, Boston's public television station, to support "Open Studio" and related arts programming.

Contents

Melodie and Cello	13
The Studio	14
Portrait	15
Apple	16
Painting	17
Light	18
No, No Breath at All	19
Poem	20
That Womb Fixed	21
Music Maker	22
Melodie	23
Wail	24
Trippin' on Rhythm	25
Babies Dancing	26
Sisters Dancing	27
Dancer's Choice	28
Dancing With God	29
Day of the Fete	30
When I Try For Color	31
Abduction at the Gardner	32
Man Achieves Flight	34
after Auden's "Musée des Beaux Arts"	35
Nascence	36
Fantasy with Strings	37
Bach's Magnificat	38
When Hell Solidified	40
Melodie's Song	41
Presto: Notes on the Kreutzer Sonata	42
Chickadee	44
Girl with Broken Pitcher	45
Voices	46
Art of the Dying Yellow Rose	48
The Palekh Icons	49
Comes a Dividing Time	50

Finding Beauty	52
The Apprentice	53
Stone	54
The Love of Shapes and Shaping	55
Shaping	56
The Stoneworker	57
Entering the Stone	58
My Wall	59
Fire and Water	60
Footpath	61
Moon Rock in a Stream	62
The Station Agent	63
A Place of Concealment	64
Act	65
Breathing in the Second Balcony:	66
Lines for a Spent Stud	66
The Poet Donates His Body to a Medical School	67
On Prospero's Shores	68
White Pine Dancer	69
My Dancing Tree	70
Dance	71
Eldersong	72
Poet	73
The Art of Beginnings	74
Seaside	75
Listen	76
A Reading	77
Two Worcester Poetry Venues	78
Need	79
Poet As Egotist	80
Katie and the Poet	81
Where He Dwells, Dwells, Dwells	82
About the Author	83

Melodie and Cello

When first they met he spoke the names: Melodie, Cello.
She heard and knew, her touch of understanding hands.
She slowly learned composure in their sweet embrace,
together played etudes in syllables too brief for speech,
improvised on colors found in margins of illuminated
books or on the lambent surfaces of grace. At times,
they played in flowered skies Chagall designed, love
held by silver strings and whispering antiphonies.
Other times they learned to understand and know the
prosody of grief, deep vibrato rung beneath, connecting
each to each, and shared the longing ache of imperfection.
When they played for others, measures of their gain
in so many of them rung, inexpressibly sustained.

The Studio

In galleries her art in graceful space
relates authentic strangeness, ways
of making reason smile faced by mystery.
Nibbling crackers and brie the people say,
Where does she get ideas like that?

Above exhausted back street shops,
generous windows face a cold north light.
Harmony swirls and stomps around the room
drawing chaos into the game like god's own choice:
not something out of nothing, only the raw things,
artless, ready to be shaped.

Slowly turn within collage of broken shapes,
statuette half awake, paints and paste, electric drill,
broad table filled with inked or molded things,
quick drawing of unfinished man, scraps
of anonymity in boxes underneath; artifacts
just suggesting plausibility.

She's in a lonely place, hovering just above ground,
trying to reach down where artifact and insight
meet, then reach the street below.

For Marjory Lehan, artist

Portrait

A rise of land like a Saxon barrow
lies strange and cool across a moor.
There, the shadowed form of one
lone tree gestures solemnly.

From where you stand on higher ground
that tree seems distant, cool. Of course,
if something in its feature stirred
in you a curious yearning, you
could thread a way through mist between
and see—but moors, for being what
they be, hardly anyone tries.

And isn't it the ordinary
way to stand aground to view
an insular tree in its unuttering
form as if it were a picture
in a gallery, and say,
"Unique, the way it captures such
a grave and sober mood," or, "How
serene the grey mist makes it seem."

Apple

So many rooms in warm and gentle
homes have dead or dying pictures
on the walls. They were artful
the day they were hung, really
pleased someone. In little time
they atrophied and died of non-
consumption. Not Mark's apple.
I smile at least twice daily passing
by. It doesn't look good enough to eat
but it has a luscious aura, something
between the idea and execution
that slipped below all surfaces,
a light that brings my eyes alive.

After a painting by Mark Curtin

Painting

Sea things,
listen how they sing
layer on layer like opaque
remains of memory and time.

You see the waves assemble
as a chorale to the moon,
and the prayers in
a perfect whorl of shell.

Sea things dark and light,
listen how they sing,
linear as whirling is,
sea things singing.

After a series of paintings by Mark Curtin

Light

Wind races wide and light across water,
glitters in ripples within a transient space;
photons splinter like glass, emerge like a
cat inside. Light lasts, becomes interior as
by a common life. See Rodin's head of a
woman lifted in *Grief.* The wonder is, she
does not appear to breathe. Yet she breathes
us into her frame, our splintered sight.

No, No Breath at All

A face of deep grief tilts
to the darkened sky,
a neck stretched taut
to where no life,
no relief in sight
inside lidded eyes.
Faint light sighs along
high cheekbones,
brow's round sides
stretch to meet
a tight crease,
a tense center.
A slightly open mouth,
unbreathing, would speak.
No, no breath at all
to release what is seen inside.
World, woman, each
turning out of reach.

After a bronze head of a woman by Auguste Rodin entitled "La Douleur" (aka Head of Sorrow or Grief); Museum of Fine Arts, Boston, MA

Poem

Shape this poem in fluted glass,
teach me to fill it with music.
Let notes flow up a
slender stem,
widen
into
wine,
kiss
each
listener's
lips and flow
unalloyed to the mind.

That Womb Fixed

Movement deep in stone,
vital shadow tight
in that womb fixed.
Struck hammer shock
taut life will shudder,
reach expectantly.

Expressed with bear's,
boa's crush
viscera rushes out,
removes all breath
does not distill.

Purple grapes crushed
give blood red wine,
pressed skins drip
clear grappa.

Music Maker

This is our compulsion,
to be sitting by a river's edge
mesmerized by light that resolves our sight,
squatting by a campfire
lured by dance of moving flame,
cozened into dreams by the light gas flickering,

standing in the sand
where the full sea heaves,
caught in the beat of a mind consuming flow.

This is our compulsion;
the animal that loves the violin
must be singing, must be singing in its cage.

Melodie

Melodie could play buffoon to make us weep,
speak *sotto voce* rage that reached the heart
as plaintive ache, make plain the dark intensity
of overwhelming grief; but in quick space
between epode and audience response, already
she had gone beyond the echoes of our walls.
She hollowed out of ageless ice a place that
glistened with mystic lights. There were echoes
there: rare music, shadows of holy thoughts,
elusive shapes that caught notes formed along
cold walls and let them drop, bedded on soft
and silent speech. Strophe, strophe, strophe,
slow, we turn and turn until we hear within.

Wail

   (a day at Preservation Hall, a New Orleans Jazz Venue)

How many endings have you seen
since you were nine?
Long time   to read
what's been hovered   under covers,
like leaves under cool   dark   springs.
How many endings have you s e e n?

Well you know it's all beginnings
in the end. Ends be leaves blown d o w n
from living trees; beginnings are them
leaves blown down l o w, s l o w song
under water where a then grows.

We listen when spring flows green,
just seems to know which way.
Oh yes it do   it seems;   but always
not quite ready for an end,   always
n e e d s what only see ms; oh yes it do.

Are you singing with me now? Are you
leaving or beginning in a mean dry time?
I won't mind,   cept singing brings
a light for dead leaves browning under
deep   cool   springs. Still sing brother, sing.

(It's called "blowin' on the embers")

Trippin' on Rhythm

1.

Shape my lines so they move through flutes,
slide inside a wide trombone, turn within
French horns to wind their mellow designs.
Tune my ear to the sound of air as it rides
over wide white pines, over waves where it
glides light as the flight of a kestrel at sea.

2.

At times crack the straight-backed line,
get tough with it. Give it a shove.
That's where stuff
too slick gets wise
and faces the music.
It's not all sweetness and Diet Lite, y'know!

3.

Some rhythms are wide, as widely spaced as two great sister ships,
one leaving Barcelona at noon, the other leaving San Francisco soon.
Over the curve of the world they've long lost sight of each other,
but they're bound to sail through some same zones in a long tale.

4.

OooEe! Don't even talk to me about dithyrambs!*

---

*dithyrambs: impassioned, even wild choral dance and song played at the
festival of Dionysus.

Babies Dancing

All the babies are dancing
night and day day and night
asleep or in the other dream
      being
        dreaming.

Babies dance light
needing only
every moment's life
for dancing delight.
Infants in
their mothers' arms
dancing in the kitchen in
their mothers' arms.

Babies dance in plain sight,
all the babies dancing,
night and day, day and night
air dancing so like light on ice.

In their delightful light
there am I
dancing dancing

Sisters Dancing

Child lithe in love with life
quick as light on ice,
flies across the edge of dawn
where the shadow lies.

She is free as singing is,
and she is moving light;
soft as sleep the fragile dance
sings along the edge of night.

Dancer's Choice

Dancers move in wings of trees
whose roots hold stones below,

Elastic light on water moves
like music where the dancers go.

The dancer's choice and perfect
grace, to touch with lightness
earthbound space.

Dancing With God

dancing is the will
to be here, there, never
where the circle ends
moving in air
that touches everything
unafraid
this is where the light is
where the dancer's choice
makes it be
see dancing in the light
your eye brings
sing the dancer's choice
into being
this is where all life is
where the dancer's choice
makes it be

Day of the Fete

Lively all down the wide market street
revelers celebrate a holy day as each
deem appropriate to aimless pleasure.
Small boys dodge in-and-out of crowds.
A young girl holds, no doubt, a holy book.
women wear their best lace; their men
are heard laughing heartily over pots of ale
and fiddlers' music fills the air.

Against the dark side of the lane three
brown clad monks, models of sobriety,
carry greens for their monastic table.
Near them, down the middle of the lane,
six bawdy revelers dance, arm-in-arm,
woman-to-man, man-to-woman linked,
eyes alive to bright holiday possibility.

In the shaded edge, the monks: one with
sober intent reads in sinless quest of holiness.
Nearest to light, linked to the eldest monk,
a young acolyte sidewise eyes the dancers
with a least seed of passive passion.
The elder monk perceives: his dark eyes
slice seeds of possibility from deep within
a brooding cowl. The young monk shrinks.

Otherwise, the street is filled with airy light
that gleams from scoured cobblestones, music,
scenes of holiday hilarity. Light and life spring
redundantly from God's own sun. Amen.

After a work of the same name by Jules Garnier

When I Try For Color

Get red on that canvas! Get red!
And yellow-orange—life!
Your colors are dead.

She's right you know.
My brush, though, it slithers into green
when red is what I mean to see.
Then, when I try a subtle slide
to pick up red the damned brush slips
on a spur of old dried paint
and comes up all amuck in gray;
or trying for a sly twist in pale gold,
it slides—I know I tried!—into blue.

But she's right.
A work of art needs life.
Nerves, it's nerves makes all the slip;
My critic's nerves are cool,
she never slips from red to blue.
She says it's all in the control. She says
my nerves spring loose and jar my aim.

It's true.
They splatter orange torment on my soul
I haven't the control for painting life.

Abduction at the Gardner

> *In 1990, thieves broke into the Isabella Stuart Gardner Museum in Boston, MA. They removed thirteen paintings— cut them right out of the frames. As of 2019, the paintings had not been recovered.*

I miss the Fishermen most, the ghost of peace
beneath the heave of boat and wave on the wild
Sea of Galilee. It got to my teenage blood years ago,
how they hung on the lines in the grip of fear
where sails whipped in wild air, how each detail
rang so true to a boy who loved the sea.

Perhaps if they stole just one I could believe,
romantically, that someone loved it so
he made a crypt, climate controlled and lit
much better than Gardner's wall; and there
he sits alone "since none puts by/ The curtain I
have drawn for you, but I,"* his selfish
satisfaction thus a little redeemed.

But they stole more: Rembrandt and Vermeer,
and other precious work, thugs who cut them from
their frames. They only saw expensive rags
a buyer might reclaim for something under market.
Ignorance of awe wed to sordid souls.

I saw blank frames and will not look again.
El Jaleo still delights, della Robbia too, hidden in
the murky hall, Raphael and all the grilled and
dark beamed sights, the chill of wonder in
sweet passage all around the atrium.

Some day before my sight is claimed by the
thief time sends at last, I hope to stand by Galilee,
rescued and returned. In that tumultuous frame
I will again see peace beneath the heaped waves.

---

*from "My Last Duchess," Robert Browning

Man Achieves Flight

> *The bombing of Guernica by German and Italian air forces was the first time civilian populations were targeted for bombing. Well known among the many bombings of civilians after that were the fire bombing of Dresden in WWII, the first use of atomic bombs in Hiroshima and Nagasaki, and the first use of napalm bombing in Vietnam.*

The cock's dark eyes awake in flight his wide
shrieks warning
shocks to come exempt no one.   Sleep
children sleep

      Dresden
      where the children melted
Sleep children sleep

      Hiroshima, Nagasaki
      human imprints on the street
Sleep children sleep

      Vietnam napalm
      running girl screaming
Sleep children sleep

Saturday night black raptors screech. Sleep
children sleep, it's
only the sound of backyard fowl in a sick dream
shrieking
only earth of feverish green and orange fright-ignited
skies
only a beast come in the night waking innocence
to die

Inspired by Pablo Picasso's *Guernica*.

after Auden's "Musée des Beaux Arts"

The masters, passionate for war, were sure.
The many cheered them on, though mothers wept
to see the young ones go.
One sunny day by consequence of Sunni fury
Private Icarus is blown skyward by a bomb,
his daring known, his death a failed adventure.
Inarticulate, amazed and gaping faces see
those shreds of color arc in a searing sky,
while over the span of sand and sea, gannets
                         called more plaintively.
In Maine his father plowed a heavy snow,
senses bedded in dense white pain;
neighbors in their pickups passed him by
and each one lightly touched the horn.
About suffering, they were never wrong…

Nascence

The wolf, when I heard her in the cold night sky,
was I longing for her call to be hung on stars,
to see it draped like a sheer sling
that held them breathlessly in place?

All that was art about that call had its making
in the desolation of a small space, an echo of
my own relentless reach, the way I try
to dress the universe in violin motifs,
the way I listen repetition into cosmic symphony,
those infinite strings that play on the minds
of dreamers confined.

Fantasy with Strings

At first it was only fear of bees that
taught me listening by the apple tree.
Then the honeyed air rustled lilac boughs,
and bullfrog bellows hung like organ notes,
a ruffled grouse drummed his mating claim,
and the rain droned monodies on broad
oak leaves. This is where the ear begins,
the music that imbues all things.

Vision sings from strings light as dreams.
The bow that draws across is made of
dragonfly wings, and many colored sound
is carried by trembling bees, by fluted
orchid songs and wind that hums among
the choral grass, our fantasies accompanied
by infinitely tiny strings.

Bach's Magnificat

Northampton State Hospital, 11-18-00:
A local artist and others arranged a multiple speaker system
inside one of the largest empty hospital buildings. The public
was invited to stand outside, walk around the building, and
listen to the Bach Magnificat. (Luke 1:46-55) The great
building seemed inhabited by ghosts, a hundred dark windows,
many broken, most of their locked grates in place,
some stone fallen to the weeds below; remains of asylum
wherein many who lived with mental pain passed their lives—
where their lives passed them by. A great crowd of people
walked from a field below to circle the building, stand below
its walls in memory of those who were prisoners within,
and listen to the canticle.

What brought a thousand supplicants
to stand in ragged weeds in a chill wind
below these grated windows?
Alone or two or three, they filed around
that high gray vault, weaving memory in
silent space below the shadowed stone.
Huddled against the autumn and the dark,
each waited for the hour when the canticle
would be sung from speakers deep within.

Some walkers knew who lived within this
massive grey unwelcoming design. Others
came with candles for the light that was denied.

David will not speak of endless years
huddled in fear; David speaks civility
when restlessness divides other minds.
Rachel asked again, "Do you believe
I was a bad mother?" Heather is gracious
far from life in cardboard crates, far from
this gray vault's interminable security.

How brave they were to leave the barren lesson
of walls, so many years schooled in isolation.
Some are gone to lasting peace: Marie who cried
and loved to hug; Kate whose highs kept her
sleepless day on day, haggard when another
mood came on; these few among the many
who endured among the huddled supplicants,
the memories of hundreds more.

    Magnificat begins

as if we stood before a massive crypt, heavy
door rolled back with this redemptive song,
to fill the wind that chilled the bones, to fill
the silent spaces with a benediction of stone.

When Hell Solidified

When Hell solidified in ice
the wail of indentured sinners stopped.

But then it found a sound that grew,
                           organ echoes deep
as notes' rebound from stone.

The hoary deeps gave vent to views
steeped in baritone sax and lonely
voices wrung
       from muted trumpets,
plain-
tive reeds
and strings.

As wind on mountains makes new sounds
music moves on fire or blue inside
       to penetrate a sorry bone
   where love is still alive.

Oh, give praise to cool, cool Hell.

For musician and jazz enthusiast, Frank "Okie" O'Connor

Melodie's Song

Someone sings the psalms you made
mourning dying light, sings the rose you
blessed by breath within a formless night.

Someone's song draws thorns from hands
that grasp the lyric briar, takes from pain
and risk of failure strings of equal fire.

Someone's song warms all your voices
struck like bells on icy nights, song of
unsaid memories where sympathy unites.

Someone's song is nature's grace dispensed
with hope and precious pain, prayer known
to those who write to sing within their chains.

Melodie, from earlier poems, is a kind of mythic figure, a muse.

Presto: Notes on the Kreutzer Sonata

I enter through deceit of few notes softly played,
faint implication of echoes far and torn,
something remembered discomposed.
Suddenly, my spirit is wrenched and drawn
as if in a funnel of air, whirling without hurt,
storm of photons, sounds of brilliant light
charged with furious action, argument,
echo straining to exceed, attraction, repulsion
clutching hands. Unable to resist, wildly drawn,
fierce in love I am storm strong.

Amazing presto coils and springs
attacks the passion piano wrings,
frenzy spilled in tense control,
pursuit of its insane design.
Ibex clash on ragged crags,
furious loves torment each other,
murderers cry out their crimes.

Consider the sonata Tolstoy heard:
piano and violin, unnaturally restrained,
soft conversation, intimation of pleasure,
an edge of betrayal just before the presto.
Still, the solemn edge of night invites…
                        then, the Presto
excites, elevates mood, as would a wild
siren song gone to storm, a boiling sea,
something short of rage. In the belly of
a bright wave a brilliant wine is tasted.
Men and women lick their lips and
                        wonder whether…

Because I was lost
the Sonata sang chaos and pain.
In my cramped heart
that rash violin breached
mute space where a stillness never was;
into them that piano's agonized run
entered like a flood of fear.
This is a thing only my heart knew,
mastery in vain silver chains
bright as smiling, dangerous
and mean.

Who knows what that composer saw
hearing his creation go where he must go,
agony of exaltation, measure of
an enchanted lover. Did he mean
much more than even he saw
when he followed his pen across the page?
I only know that two mute listeners,
signing across time,
know the presto by heart.

Violin Sonata No. 9, "Kreutzer" by Beethoven. Tolstoy wrote a novella named after Beethoven's piece and set it in a ballroom.

Chickadee

Watch the black-capped chickadee;
your eyes will flicker to follow
her quick and undulating flight, so
like a line of quarter notes in the sky,
but it's not the song you hear her sing.
No matter what notes you may see,
for her it's a trick of evasive flight,
a way to save her life.

Girl with Broken Pitcher

A shattered pitcher
dropped by Cynthia, ten last May.
Today is a day that will not end
until a pillow's sympathy.
It isn't sorrow in her eyes,
nor resolution in her hands
(clenched and twisted in her lap).
Her fears are quieter than sighs,
a trembling wing inside.

Nearby, a shattered vision
hovers above herself, cracked and dry,
signifying innocence burned inside,
empathetic impulse sucked away
in the flame of sharing lives.
A man is gone again, rides old
pickups into the sun, bottle
at his side. The vision lies
all through a long, mean evening.

After *The Broken Picture,* a painting by artist William A. Bougereau, in the California Palace of the Legion of Honor

Voices

In unquiet silence she explains,

I am not sure you are to be trusted,
the voice that searches within.

Yes, I begin to see. You are plain.
Your dress, like all the rest,
a plain disguise. An eyelid
very slightly droops, suggesting
imperfection. Your demeanor:
hands folded quietly in your lap,
the slight inward tilt of your body,
the artless waiting in your eyes,
a statement held in reserve.

I am waiting for your silence to take
the shape either of listening
or of something else.

I see that you have history within,
not just your own, reservoir of doubt,
reserve that could spill into fear.
You do this with perfect calm,
experience of ages passed intact.

You presume.

Nature and nurture, but I see
that it's not about speech.

Perhaps. It is still too soon.

Poem suggested by *Girl With A Blue Dress,* ceramic by Kiki Smith, in the Worcester Art Museum, Worcester, MA. (The girl, about age ten or twelve, has not been given a name.)

Art of the Dying Yellow Rose

A rose is beautiful, yes,
but why paint flowers, why
imitate the dying light
along the wilted edge
where yellow fades?—
too much like feeling ice
in the edges of age—
the way you've caught it, withering,
just enough
to please.

I was turning away,
as from an old man's story,
conceded to be true but too
familiar to excite another time;
but just as unexpected silence
gives voice another life
I caught some light
you almost rubbed away, colors
of a layered life, where
nearly muted as a hidden grief
in texture of delight, your art
survived the palette knife.

After a painting by Mark Curtin

The Palekh Icons

Religions live in deep appeal to needs that Nature
        leaves unsealed, open wounds
that have no sure relief, that only love sees.
        Children of time's untamed place.
The Palekh Icons come from centuries of this
        desire to be contained in peace
among these figures painted wise and kind,
their sympathy for sorrow.
These ordinary faces from the villages from
        Antioch to Moscow, ancient
reaches North and East, faces brown as
        farmers, artisans, those eyes
that sign a patient look of service, sacrifice,
lives that held the people tight.

One of the world's largest collections of Russion icons can be viewed at the Museum of Russian Icons in Clinton, MA

Comes a Dividing Time

Root constricted blooms left
in old clay pots, letters tied
in ribbon in a cedar box,
snow-blue shadows
on a January night.

Across the river
harvest moon eases
through the spruce thick hill,
softly lights the ice-covered river
and fills her wide windowed room.

She remembers when they both agreed openness is right,
their design to bring both light and hillside in,
themselves be windows into sight.

She sits, now, with the moon across her lap
listening to other nights when they were
silent in each other's arms, floated up
and through the windowed wall,
figures in a picture by Chagall.

I   was thinking of Marc Chagall

                    When   Y O U
        Entered

    Oh   i
            slipped   the paperflowered walls
                                behind
L O V E

                looked   browneyed
                                                daisies

                        At   Y O U   Dancing

        in (our)

                    sunstar moonroom sky
                                        Oh
                                            L O V E

Finding Beauty

A great blue heron glides along the river,
solemn form in perfectly balanced flight.
All that perfection of grace and I'm not
reminded of prayer. Why do I see pterosaur,
bat wing, serpentine predator, gray fear that
leads to thought of small things under mud?

In crystal dew the pitcher plant, spider waits
on silver silk, puma sleek on hemlock limb;
next of kin, beauty of all efficient things.
Stalking: how beautiful waiting can seem.
Glides to a stop without stirring the water,
waits, still as the Giacometti near the Goya.

The Apprentice

He painted me slashes of dark and bright. The man
saw things that way, as if we were martyrs held in place
with lead set in windows on the dark side of a church.
I sat patiently while he worked, then left without
a word. I suppose he meant he said it all in colors.

But that mark of Cain across the brow, the slash
of blue? And why the green-black background,
dark as a gorge far down in the sea? It feels
like a time before I was born, or maybe a place
that follows death. Somehow, I feel it held me
prisoner, molded forever in lead, or sin.

Those heavy strokes of blue and black, those are
the bones that ring my eyes like lines that rise
from buried life, sight in one sliver of light
deep in a blue-black cave—it could be the eye
of a secret beast—as if to hide the worst of me
from me (Or is it himself?) Surely I'm hearing
the shape of my own blue fears! Why look, the
jaunty rake of my hat. And isn't that the very line
of reverence around the mouth? I think that speaks
what he meant to say. Yes! Reverence
            Still, I wonder about the eyes.

After a lithograph by Georges Rouault, viewed at a special exhibition
(December 2012-March 2013) at the Worcester Art Museum, Worcester, MA

Stone

Some form is deep in the stone.
Tight in that womb fixed
is shadow as vital as flight.

Struck hammer shock alive
it will sing taut lift and reach,
shuddering expectantly.

The Love of Shapes and Shaping

First a face, so early I have no memory,
one of those warm shapes that shaped
a safe and happy time before time began.

When there was time—at first it only moved
in the brilliant shapes of holidays—our
kitchen and the windows shaped the day.

Later came free shapes of cats, trees, rivers,
falling snow, herons and crows tossed in
invisible wind, all that moves outside of me.

                  In time I made some shapes from shapes I drew
together, red and blue and stone, places in
my dreams and weave of things I could not see.

I learned that songs have shapes, that shapes
are formed behind the eyes, in mirrors rising
out of mind's electric beauty, new.

Shaping

Maybe in your artist's mind
you have seen a stone
with a boy inside, daring you
to cut away what twisted grain
the heat and cooling made,
as Michelangelo saw David
and brought him into view.

But have you seen a child
with a stone inside, annealed
in the usual way: slow cooling
after shapes are formed in heat.
And when the burden cools
unseen in that dark cavity
it sits in a loaded sling.

The Stoneworker

That ragged heap of stone behind the shed
is, in my plan a simple wall, a gray mosaic
I and others will admire set beside
a footworn path, and made just for appeal
to sense of rugged touch, not to divide
like walls we make with supple words.

In a day as good as any before the sun
tops the hill I lace good boots and go
with cart and crowbar, feeling agreeably merged,
aesthete and troglodyte, and haul the many-sized
stone to where the work begins.

My hands seem primitive claws that curl
on ragged stone. I lift and feel the pull
on shoulders, biceps, work of heart and lungs,
rush of dopamine, adrenaline and sweat
upon my neck. My belly flexes when
the heavy rock presses in. I pick the way
in heavy tread to where the wall begins
and drop it on that holy spot.

All day the work goes on, the artist mind
selecting and the ox-like troglodyte
plodding, stone on stone. After each new
load is set I rest a bit and think of Sisyphus*,
his momentary ease atop the hill.

---

*Reference to the last line in Camus' essay, *The Myth of Sisyphus*,
"Il faut imaginer Sisyphe heureux"

Entering the Stone

This shape, not that, is this rock's phrasing,
lines that follow unseen grains.

Pursuit of inward shapes is much like
being alone by the sea on a moonlit night
trying to follow movement of a diving seal.
You know its sleek black lines are tighter
than any words can say, ligaments and skin
that move like water itself, and yet you know
it will appear again, not quite like waves
but blending well.

A space within you knows and waits.

                        Suddenly
The chisel sings, shaving even memory or
symmetry away when they divide the eye,
discarding what would firmly hold,
perhaps has claim to its own space,
except you see another phrasing here,
and that holds all of stone
you care to know.

Sculptor and poet work alike: listening with patient attention, looking for the life inside, loving the right mistakes, loving shapes.

My Wall

Old bricks stamped with a mill's mark, a gift to me,
or I took it as my own. Well, both then.
I thought to face it with authentic design in clay I dug alone.

Long days I came to the pit where clay was mined.
I gathered hair from anywhere it freely fell and mixed it
with moistened clay, agglutinate of forms, articulation of intent.

By hand and eye I kneaded and applied the heavy stuff, raw
to my touch. Course on course of rough shaped clay held
by gravity, by infiltration, grain to grain on porous brick,

imprint of stroke and stress, whorl and ridge and palm,
every layer an attempt of infinite density in a small space,
peculiar space holding itself in place, only needing a shape of light.

When all was dried (air and time and grit set down as history)
patterns never planned arose, texture of memory surprised,
shapes of light; like all becoming, strange. I say my work is done;

but time, dust, air, particles of vagrant life arrive and cling,
ions bond and subtle strokes of chemistry work their tiny hands.
New shapes bleed from underneath, lines that intersect, even
names

arise, embrace, couple with wall, another life to rise and fall.
Earth and time on lines of stress, where elegant cracks redesign.
This wall of mine.

Inspired by work of artist Andy Goldsworthy

Fire and Water

rise and die so quick. Eyelids flicker
and all is new, bright inconstant shapes,
forever in and out of sight, renewed
until mingled with mind along the spine.
Serene excitement, like how the last
moments of dying light ease the mind.

Artists hold them still; still we see whirl,
unsteady shapes we recreate, reflected heat,
synaptic space, blood's need unimpeded.
Something in fire that satisfies,
something in water's glide and flight,

desire's rise and fall, twisting shape of life,
like fear and elation in love, abandonment
and love in grief, like small daily alienation
and connection that leaves us tired by night.

A sweeter peace arrives, held by moving shapes
that stay in place, for once do not sear or
suffocate, fascination of death undying.

Inspired by work of artist Andy Goldsworthy

Footpath

ice

Cloud shapes reshape light,
hush remaining marigold's eye.
Vapor's gray airway layers,
seep.
Ice airs, sucked and shoved eel shape
south and east, nuzzle wet morning slope,
slip into pores shaped by rock and worm and breathing.
Ice shape
inside epidermal springs
lift the footpath where the shod foot goes.

heat

Clouds blow east or dissipate, leave transient space,
diamonds crack on pitted rock, silver streaks split,
gravitate, ooze in earth, breath
under rock drowns, moved
               and moving things
seek darkness
underneath with seed.   White veins
break and green, run for their lives
in muck where the shod foot goes.

Inspired by work of artist Andy Goldsworthy

Moon Rock in a Stream

Settle in soft indenture on the bank.
Look where the white rock folds and braids the water,
stays the rapid weave of light.

Instant bits of diamond white glitter
along the rolling break where water and the white
moon stone collide.

Light flecks rise from all its satellites; pebbles
slick black, red or white gathered by the moon's flow
roll in syncopated time.

A shadow moves its dark across, veils
the whiteness in a muted motion, passes from the sky,
moon emerges from a dark womb.

At rest the white moon moves, reflects
on every restless drop, serene in the weave
of impatient cradled motion.

The mossy bank where you lie cool slips into mist,
and world smoothly moves.

Inspired by work of artist Andy Goldsworthy

The Station Agent

It's a dream scene, Chagall and time
having writ the usual confusion into
states of mind.
The dancers' moves are tied by signs to
switches, destinations.
They follow the train's incoming light
where it tracks the rails,
find a relation between time and sight.
As the train arrives
the pas de deux grows less intense,
less sure of grace.
The station agent properly pays attention
to relations;
the adagio is gracefully declined in favor
of a gesture
that draws the eye to a steady line of light
along the rails.
As dancers take positions for the coda
the station agent stands aside.

---

a fragment (could be travelers watching a train arrive or leave)

A Place of Concealment

Act I

My *genre* here is comedy, a term generic
wherein I, hardly *sui generis,* play at hiding,
hide at playing. Unembarrassed, unashamed,
I play a simple fool—nothing at all like you;
or confidant to a luckless lover, giving him
advice he trusts, while I, by doting on her
ample bust, urge both he and you to lust.
I sometimes play a choral role, clown endowed
with echo lines that mock a villain's crimes
with a stock of easy rhymes. I knew you
wouldn't mind.
I'm just mimesis in disguise. I don't apologize.

Act II

I slide with a wink of the eye to satire,
the *genre,* I protest, I find far more than jest.
You think you see in me a neighbor
or your husband's silly vice, see a foolish
cleric's folly, sneer at vain effete pretension—
never an extension of yourself. I delight
in these deceptions wherein all my skill resides;
it's just that I have analyzed the sober lies
wherein we hide. I show you these in comic guise,
but all the while my eye is on the honest enterprise.
My purpose all subliminal is to reveal the criminal
with lines that lightly moralize, that lightly moralize.*
I'm just mimesis in disguise. I don't apologize.

---

*I don't apologize to Sir William S. Gilbert (Gilbert & Sullivan) for appropriating this line.

Act

What of the singer who
won't go on the stage, who
abstains from being scenery?

There's no special time for turning,
for solitary compact with the dark—
divined by priest, psychiatrist, mother.

But there it is, just offstage,
the dark. Not even a cue occurs,

There is music fills within cannot
bear sharing until it spends itself
in one inaudible line.

Breathing in the Second Balcony:
Lines for a Spent Stud

It's the oldest drama.
You'd think I'd know the play by heart,
having played the stage hand's and the usher's part;
but I have not that painful-joyful memory
carried growing through the wonder time.
Only a distant envy. Still,
I am filled with wonder at the scene
and always rise to give applause.

Now let's see if I can follow the lines.
I'm in the second balcony, of course.
Impressive height, but the air is thin
and it's so difficult to catch the inner action.
In the ensemble scenes I'm fine,
identifying all the roles of those who serve.
But for the close-ups: the recognition scene,
secrets played before the mirror,
the carriage of joyful pride in the long walk
across the stage, the heady merge of two roles;
for these and others—which I cannot remember,
being so far away and knowing so few lines—
I need instruction, X-ray, infrared, an annotated text.
Such aids as these conceive in me—eh—
the play's scenario, its palpitating memory,
except, of course, the wondrous birthing pain,
the breathing infant at the breast, nourishing again.

The curtain closes on the final scene, and I go down
to haul the props that all pack horses
have been trained to do. I do not dare to utter neigh.

The Poet Donates His Body to a Medical School

An anatomic gift, a bit of thrift, Horatio,
my wedded parts disjoined to grace
an antiseptic table, to give an earnest
acolyte a hands-on try to learn (sans my
undeserved complaints) hidden signs
of brief humanity's interior design.
There'll be no ghost to haunt the stage,
no sentient threat or plea for sympathy.
And when my bones teach nothing new,
in memory my too too disembodied self
(except within the urn upon the shelf)
will now and then appear in unintended
stealth—perchance in some poor poet's
metered dream. He'll view what's left
and say, Alas, poor man, I knew his
brief tirades when he began to strut his
verse upon the stage. O God, how weary,
stale, flat—and most of all, unprofitable—
his too-too-heavy lines upon the page.

—Curt Curtin, patient poet

On Prospero's Shores

Slower than the measured tide we dance,
turn and turn with yearning in our eyes
and fire in us warmer than the sands
all cradled in a round embracing sky.
Together we stand naked by the sea,
we two alone. Your hands reach up, caress,
my hands reach low to press soft flesh to me
while sun and air upon us warmly rest.
Within us nature's buoyant aim is formed,
an ever moving tide where love's redeemed.
That song that made the lovers' dance be born
was made of nature's trust in lover's dreams;
for we are made, in Prospero's design,
to seek the risk of dance that measures time.

White Pine Dancer

White pine branches layered long and light

in lift the wind song plays.
White pine dancer gestures ritual of flight,
or signs like a Balinese dancer's hands.
      Look to where the gesture stops,
      our share of lightness caught
      in earth and root and rock.

My Dancing Tree

is one inverted root
in a window hung where startled birds
fly by, mystified.
Wild and hairy, she has come
from struggle underneath,
a darkness she alone
can exorcise.
Her only queer deformity
is in her feet, it seems;
but that is where her memory resides.
She means to say:

With these cramped feet I spring
from darkness to my wide design
lighter than the gritted city air.
I had to break my heart away
from dark that held me there; so
you can see these feet and shins
and knees are bent to spring, and
I can be a flower or an orison,
such spring that teases all that
lives in air like wind and sleet;
and Ah, what this has made of me:
a city's window tree that ballerinas
in their dreams
        of   mastery
              could wish to be.

Note: The author occasionally creates root sculptures.

Dance

Before imagination drew on stony walls,
before the metaphor was measured for
the listening clan, one who would
in time design these things leapt and
ran; whirling, felt the untaught body's
sweet release from all that pulls to ground.

Knee raised high and downward pointed toe,
symmetry of stilted bird against a silent
night; or wild excitement, turning, turning,
hair in swirl of stormy trees, body's
echo and response to all the dancer sees.

Make a story spun of love, fast and slow,
but burning, one that leaps with giddy
lightness, spins in dizzy sweet elation,
life expressed in rhythmic affirmation.

Make a white robed circle whirl, ceremony
stolen from the mystery of night, lithe arm
lit by the footlight fire where the hand
signs grace to the hands that flicker in night.

Eldersong

Dance however you care
dare the steps they said
were done. Undo the wraps
of words that cover your
best song. That voice is wrong
that offers you no dancing song
and bids you sit among
the long dull row beside
the hall to watch the young
gavotte and reel. You feel
a rich and deep cadenza, long
as need be for the song
you rung along the years.

Poet

Merely a plain fool—
No cap-a-bells and somersaults,
adroit advisor to kings,
pleased with secret influence
and glad for the quick wit
that keeps a fool alive—No,
I stumble across the stage
looking for pearls I dropped,
a clumsy string of words that ring
no bells in the towers of the wise.

And yet I cannot help but try,
trying as it is to be a lame fool.
Somewhere in this scenery of
yearning, fear, a touch of love,
I still believe a simple measure
wrought from all the broken songs
will sing a grace so plain
that fools will know it as their own.

The Art of Beginnings

My job is to polish a long, winding stair rail.
Marks of many hands, ones that leave sweat,
others that seem to leave nothing, each
alter my purpose, but only if
I get the touch, feel the need.
My fingers move until I find resistance,
however slight. Whatever resists interests.
I begin from the bottom stair,
where each resistance is another beginning.
It helps to sing. Anything at first, what comes.
Sing tooral i ooral i ooral i ay. There's a measure.
Buff and look, a bit of spit, buff and look.
Try not to look to the top;
jobs like this get tedious when you try to see
all at once. This job does not call for
excessive executive drive,
immediate need to reach the top.
There are those who say
they have done the whole thing at a rush.
They sit astride and ride down all the way,
Wheeee!
That won't get the real under side.

Seaside

Listen: a sinuous baritone sings
       somewhere below the range
       of dwarf pines by the sea,
       variations riffed on seaborne air
       skimmed from deeps
       beneath comprehension.

Mesmerized by rhythms larger
       than any spit of land that claims
       commensurate effect—purpose,
       power, identity—

We strain to sing:
       oboes, cellos, late night sets
       of baritone sax & meditation,
       even a deep organ stop
       that imitates gods or seasons,

It's where we are, babe, roots in sand
made to suck life from roots at sea.

Listen

It is ear that teaches song—
touch loves itself too much
and taste is easily satisfied.
Vision waits upon aftersong.

We need to hear the phrase, the
measure of essential grace
that echoes common song; in this,
a hint of universal harmony,
a hint of chaos in delight.

And when we have it rich in hand,
in measures we deliciously repeat,
we know no fear of bonded life
under lines of human sight.

Song survives our brief restraint;
when the wind sings it whirls
it into a new thing: birdsong,
lavender innuendo over the bay,
grave hum in salt marsh sedge—music
that moves like endless play of
light singing in the restless ear
of earthbound night.

A Reading

We came to hear you read, asking
only bring us sound and sense.

When you have found your voice
let us hear you twice, and let us
see it on the page until it grows,
then let us hear you read again.

We also grow, though ours a private
and supportive role, act of inner
breath with you, word and word and
breath, inbreathing song, hearing
whole what we mean in this reach.

Two Worcester Poetry Venues

Cool Beans

Reading this inside a juke box
makes me feel like writing similes
all over wild and multi-colored walls:
"Cool Bean walls are painted green
as train station urinals,"
"Cool Bean Art is full of mirth,
wild as elephant afterbirth."
Without a doubt it has a strong effect
I'm feeling like a mixed metaphor
choking an unkind editor.

Poets' Parlor, Sturbridge

It's more like a nest or a place
on the needle soft forest floor
where serene people nestle in
to listen and read.
In this small space warm faces
wait within reach, as if
the touch of each word's feeling
held not only hearts in
sympathy but took them
by the hands as well.

With thanks to several Worcester county poetry venues that welcomed the author for readings.

Need

I have heard the poets read their hearts,
expecting the pardon of art in little rooms
already surfeited with others' expectations.
I have seen the artists linger at an opening,
appraise the eyes that glance and wander by
or stay to give implicit benediction.

Art for art's sake? Over a glass of wine, perhaps,
and yes, in the lonely space until the work is done;
but after that the maker too much mourns
if art sleeps easy on an unread page or stacked
in the dark back room, inviting only memory's eyes.

Let the still life lie. Go now to the lonely space
that fills desire with writhing lines; they grow
in the sweet ache that has no expectations.

Poet As Egotist

His ego was an invasive plant. Little by little,
it edged forget-me-nots away. He became
increasingly contained within one garden,
unrestrained. It started when a bird bestowed
a seed, a gift of admiration for a leaf he hung
upon a tree. Oh, the lure of birds that dropped
their seeds into his garden! He grew a green
epitheliomal blossom on his thumb. He thought
it was harmless because when he sucked it
tasted so like the succulent taste of praise and
brought hallucinatory blossoms to the mind.
He dreamed of being a garden that would
echo the sun and shine like exotic knives.
He dreamed he wore robes of honeycombs
knitted with only the lines he spoke to
compensate the drones, and people licked
his knees when he was alone on a podium.
Oh, the soul that grows alone on a podium!

Katie and the Poet

Isn't he grand?
The man has such a way with words,
how they flow like god's own thoughts
from somewhere you wouldn't be likely to know.
And he does it all with bits of talk
scattered around like a broken mirror
instead of a sentence you could read all at once.

It's deep he is,
and learned in things you wouldn't understand
any more than a goat in church.

Ah, but wasn't that a grand poem he wrote,
full of words that I haven't heard more than
twice in my life.
And he read it all with such wonderful feeling,
you'd swear to god he was a priest.

My Tim was making eyes all the while,
but I can tell you I was deeply moved.
The whole thing just flowed, like water over a bog,
a river of words and not a one of them too plain.
I wasn't all that sure of his meaning, but
I get the drift, as they say of fog in the morning.
We shouldn't be too proud, you see,
pretending to know all the deep things
a man like that could say.

Still, I wonder, does he talk that way all the time?
It must be a fine headache for his wife
to be always thinking,
what does he mean?
and does he expect an answer?

Where He Dwells, Dwells, Dwells

A question now arises that it seems
we must decide as to ownership of
poets of some fame. Who will get to
put a plaque or a plague on a doorway,
who will bring a city literary names?
Does it matter if the poets left to find
a better life, or arrived for a while
on vacation; it is still considered right
that the city claim a site they ennobled
with their presence and their fame.
Literati who apprise from the cities
far and wide where the poet may
have dwelled, since he died—was it
Baltimore or Boston or some other place
that lost him? Does the bleating heart
reside under civic boards who prize
a connection with a poet's predilection
for dissection? Is his reputation swelled
by what a city's claim impels; or is
clamor and the clanging all their
monody compels?

About the Author

Curt Curtin is a lifelong poet with three self-produced chapbooks and many individual poems appearing in journals and other publications. In 2005 he was the recipient of the Jacob Knight Award for Poetry and in 2010, received the Frank O'Hara Poetry award. He won second place in the 2019 annual contest of the Connecticut Poetry Society, and two other poems were selected for publication in an Irish anthology, *Writing Home: The 'New Irish' Poets* (Dedalus Press, 2019). Curt has been a featured reader in many poetry venues in Massachusetts and New Hampshire, and twice in Ireland. *For Art's Sake* is his first full-length collection.

Originally from Boston, Curt lived in Western Massachusetts for many years, including a year living alone in the Berkshire woods. He taught literature and creative writing for 20 years at Westfield State University and currently dwells in Worcester, Massachusetts, with his wife, Dee O'Connor.

www.ingramcontent.com/pod-product-compliance
Lightning Source LLC
Chambersburg PA
CBHW021023090426
42738CB00007B/877